THE JUDGE
LESSONS ON CHRISTIAN EDUCATION

THE NAMES OF CHRIST ILLUSTRATED

ACTIVITY BOOK

THE NOC ILLUSTRATED ACTIVITY BOOKS: AN AMAZING WAY TO TEACH YOUTH THE MANY DIFFERENT CHARACTERS OF CHRIST FOUND IN THE HOLY SCRIPTURES.

ISBN: 1-441-46174-4

PRINTED IN THE UNITED STATES OF AMERICA

COVER PAGE DESIGNED BY DYNAMIC ANIMATION PRODUCTIONS, LLC

PREFACE

"HENCEFORTH THERE IS LAID UP FOR ME A CROWN OF RIGHTEOUSNESS, WHICH THE LORD, THE RIGHTEOUS JUDGE, SHALL GIVE ME AT THAT DAY: AND NOT TO ME ONLY, BUT UNTO ALL THEM ALSO THAT LOVE HIS APPEARING." 2 TIMOTHY 4:8 (KJV)

TO OUR PARENTS, TEACHERS AND GUARDIANS: IT IS A PRIVILEGE TO STUDY GOD'S WORD WITH YOUR CHILDREN AND A BLESSING TO TRAIN AND DISCIPLINE THEM FOR SERVICE IN THE MASTER'S CAUSE. ALONG WITH THEIR BIBLES, WE STRONGLY ENCOURAGE YOUR PARTICIPATION IN THE CHILD'S USAGE OF THIS ACTIVITY BOOK.

BASIC EDUCATION
CROSSWORD PUZZLE 1

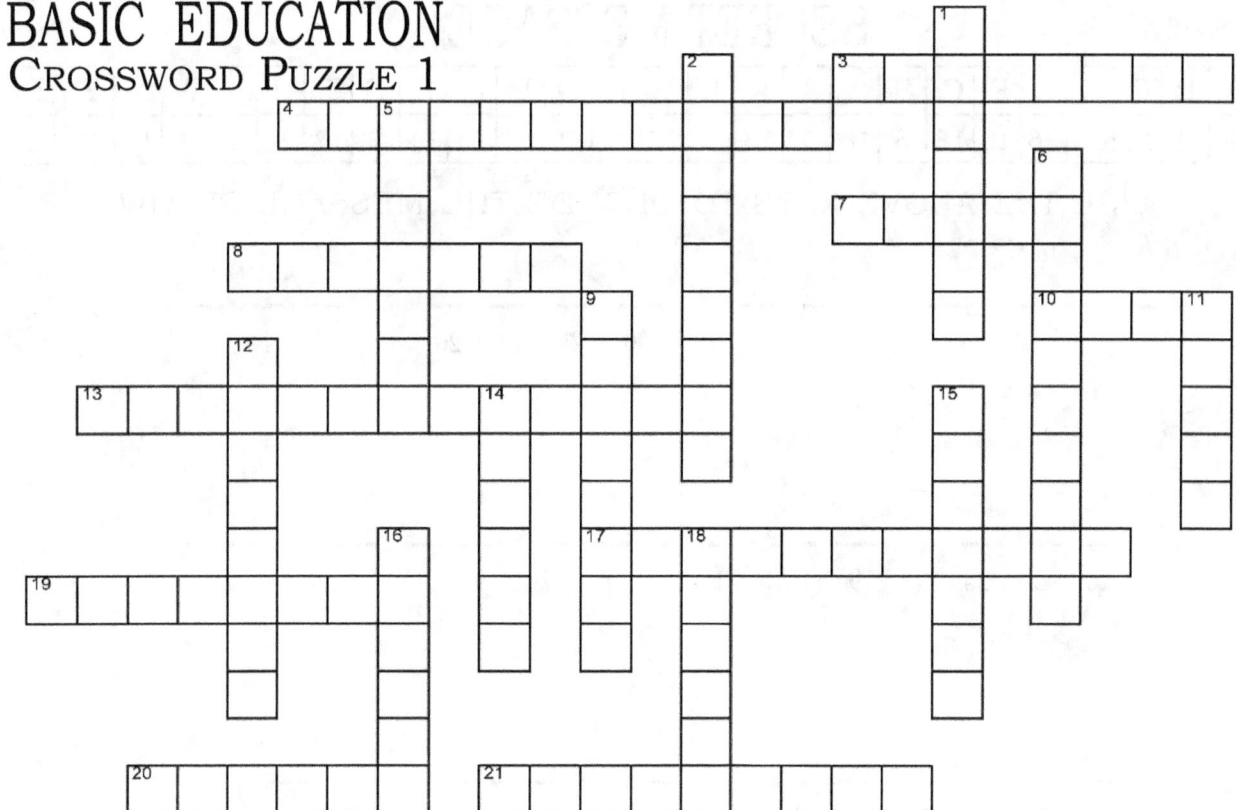

ACROSS

3. TO DWELL ON ANYTHING IN THOUGHT; TO CONTEMPLATE; TO STUDY; TO TURN OR REVOLVE ANY SUBJECT IN THE MIND.

4. CONTROL OBTAINED BY ENFORCING COMPLIANCE OR ORDER. INSTRUCTED; EDUCATED; SUBJECTED TO RULES AND REGULATIONS; CORRECTED; CHASTISED; PUNISHED; ADMONISHED.

7. THAT SOFT WHITISH MASS ENCLOSED IN THE CRANIUM OR SKULL.

8. TO EXAMINE AND GRASP THE MEANING OF WRITTEN OR PRINTED CHARACTERS, WORDS, OR SENTENCES.

10. A MEANS OF DETERMINING THE PRESENCE, QUALITY, OR TRUTH OF SOMETHING; A TRIAL.

13. COMPREHENDING; APPREHENDING THE IDEAS OR SENSE OF ANOTHER, OR OF A WRITING; LEARNING OR BEING INFORMED. KNOWING.

17. A CUSTOM, PRACTICE, RELATIONSHIP, OR BEHAVIORAL PATTERN OF IMPORTANCE IN THE LIFE OF A COMMUNITY OR SOCIETY.

19. ONE WHO EMBRACES AND ASSISTS IN SPREADING THE TEACHINGS OF ANOTHER. ONE OF THE ORIGINAL FOLLOWERS OF JESUS.

20. TO MAKE AN EFFORT TO HEAR SOMETHING. TO HEARKEN; TO GIVE EAR.

21. THE ABILITY TO LEARN AND REASON; THE CAPACITY FOR KNOWLEDGE AND UNDERSTANDING. THE ABILITY TO THINK ABSTRACTLY OR PROFOUNDLY.

DOWN

1. TO BRING UP, AS A CHILD; TO INSTRUCT; TO INSTILL INTO THE MIND PRINCIPLES OF ARTS, SCIENCE, MORALS, RELIGION AND BEHAVIOR.

2. THE SUM OR RANGE OF WHAT HAS BEEN PERCEIVED, DISCOVERED, OR LEARNED. LEARNING.

5. A PERSON ENGAGED IN STUDY; ONE WHO IS DEVOTED TO LEARNING, EITHER IN A SCHOOL, COLLEGE, UNIVERSITY, OR IN PRIVATE.

6. A TEACHER; A PERSON WHO IMPARTS KNOWLEDGE TO ANOTHER BY PRECEPT OR INFORMATION.

9. TO HAVE OR FORMULATE IN THE MIND. TO REASON ABOUT OR REFLECT ON; PONDER. HAVING IDEAS; IMAGINING.

11. TO IMPART KNOWLEDGE OR SKILL TO. TO PROVIDE KNOWLEDGE OF; INSTRUCT IN.

12. TO GAIN KNOWLEDGE, COMPREHENSION, OR MASTERY OF THROUGH EXPERIENCE OR STUDY. TO FIX IN THE MIND OR MEMORY.

14. A WORD THAT COMPREHENDS ALL THE WORKS OF GOD; THE UNIVERSE.

15. TO FORM (LETTERS, WORDS, OR SYMBOLS) ON A SURFACE SUCH AS PAPER WITH AN INSTRUMENT SUCH AS A PEN.

16. A PORTION OF A BOOK OR MANUSCRIPT ASSIGNED BY A TEACHER TO A PUPIL TO BE LEARNED, OR FOR AN EXERCISE.

18. A PLACE OF EDUCATION, OR COLLECTION OF PUPILS, OF ANY KIND.

CROSSWORD PUZZLE 1: ANSWERS FOUND ON PAGE 36

SECRET MESSAGE 1

A	B	C	D	E	F	G	H	I	J	K	L	M	N	O	P	Q	R	S	T	U	V	W	X	Y	Z
9	4	15	21	26	10	18	5	16	1	13	6	23	8	2	14	24	11	3	17	25	7	19	12	20	22

USE THE ABOVE KEYS TO DECODE THE MESSAGE BELOW

T A K E   M Y   Y O K E   U P O N
17 9 13 26   23 20   20 2 13 26   25 14 2 8

Y O U ,   A N D   L E A R N   O F
20 2 25   9 8 21   6 26 9 11 8   2 10

M E ;   F O R   I   A M   M E E K
23 26   10 2 11   16   9 23   23 26 26 13

A N D   L O W L Y   I N   H E A R T :
9 8 21   6 2 19 6 20   16 8   5 26 9 11 17

A N D   Y E   S H A L L   F I N D
9 8 21   20 26   3 5 9 6 6   10 16 8 21

R E S T   U N T O   Y O U R   S O U L S .
11 26 3 17   25 8 17 2   20 2 25 11   3 2 25 6 3

WHERE IS THIS TEXT FOUND: _____

UNSCRAMBLE THE WORDS BELOW
THEN UNSCRAMBLE THE MISSING LETTERS FOR THE WORD BELOW

LOWGE<u>E</u>NDK   _____

DISRUNATEG_DN   _____

RE_LN   _____

HAT_CERE   _____

OSMI_W   _____

UTTONSINTI_   _____

GRI_WIN   _____

SHIRT_Y   _____

N_TDSET   _____

TRUENA   _____

<u>E</u> __ __ __ __ __ __ __ __

UNSCRAMBLE EXERCISE 1: ANSWERS FOUND ON PAGE 37

"FINDING HIS WAY IS KEY IN THE WORD OF GOD"
SEEK AND FIND YOUR WAY THROUGH THE MAZE BELOW

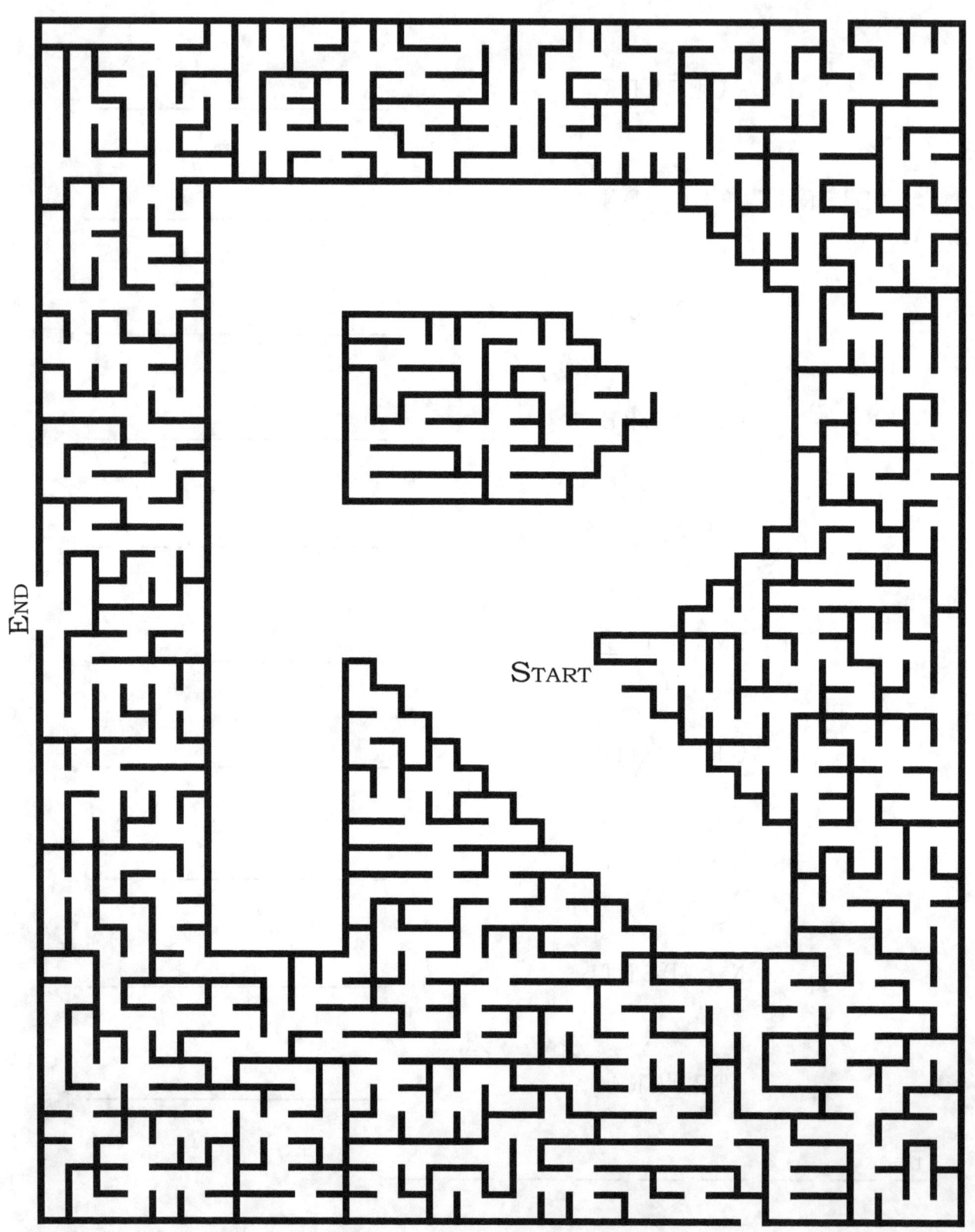

4

SEE HOW MANY WORDS
YOU CAN MAKE OUT OF
EDUCATION

"AND THOU SHALT TEACH THEM ORDINANCES AND LAWS, AND SHALT SHEW THEM THE WAY
WHEREIN THEY MUST WALK, AND THE WORK THAT THEY MUST DO."
~ EXODUS 18:20

LINE UPON LINE, PRECEPT UPON PRECEPT, HERE A LITTLE, THERE A LITTLE...

WRITE DOWN YOUR UNDERSTANDING OF THESE VERSES

DEUTERONOMY 6:6-9

_____

_____

PROVERBS 22:6

_____

_____

1 CORINTHIANS 15:10

_____

_____

1 CORINTHIANS 2:1-5

_____

_____

EPHESIANS 4:13

_____

_____

PROVERBS 3:5-6

_____

_____

DANIEL 1:1-21

_____

_____

CHRISTIAN EDUCATION
FIND THESE WORDS IN THE FOREST OF LETTERS

```
F Z L N P G X L J D G T U V Y X B V M T O L P S T
B M U A P M O X T N I N V Y B V D T E S U R C O X
H Z X Z X O C N I T H S E M I E U P D O N V F S T
I T Q P H N H N A E E V C A Y C B Y I F D K Y I B
B N V C R V R W G T A A M I M X O A T B E F T Q Q
P D S G E A S Z D L U N C S P D L H A R R C M D Z
X R X T E D V M Q T R R Y H O L X V T I S C H I G
O E W L I I U H C V U B E Z S S E S E N T G M S S
S A X L V T K C U Z J Z C L D Q V C V S A W F C K
T D N T H K U X A Y I N T E L L E C T T N W I I C
U I R X H H N T O T W B Y P T J L P O R D Z K P K
D N A J V I L X I T E L F P E W A W N U I D Y L M
E G Y Q A K N I R O V E W F S T Z V E C N V L I V
N T Y R R X X K S J N W R I T I N G I T G L E N E
T U B N Q I F L I T R L D C W G N E V O R S Q E K
Q X F R L E S S O N E B K S W E T V L R M E E D E
T L D O U F M I H P G N S Z J K N O W L E D G E U
```

KNOWLEDGE	LEARNING	TEACH
STUDENT	SCHOOL	TEST
UNDERSTANDING	DISCIPLE	DISCIPLINED
READING	WRITING	LISTEN
NATURE	LESSON	BRAIN
THINKING	INTELLECT	EDUCATE
INSTITUTION	INSTRUCTOR	MEDITATE

WORD SEARCH 1: ANSWERS FOUND ON PAGE 35

7

COLORING ACTIVITY

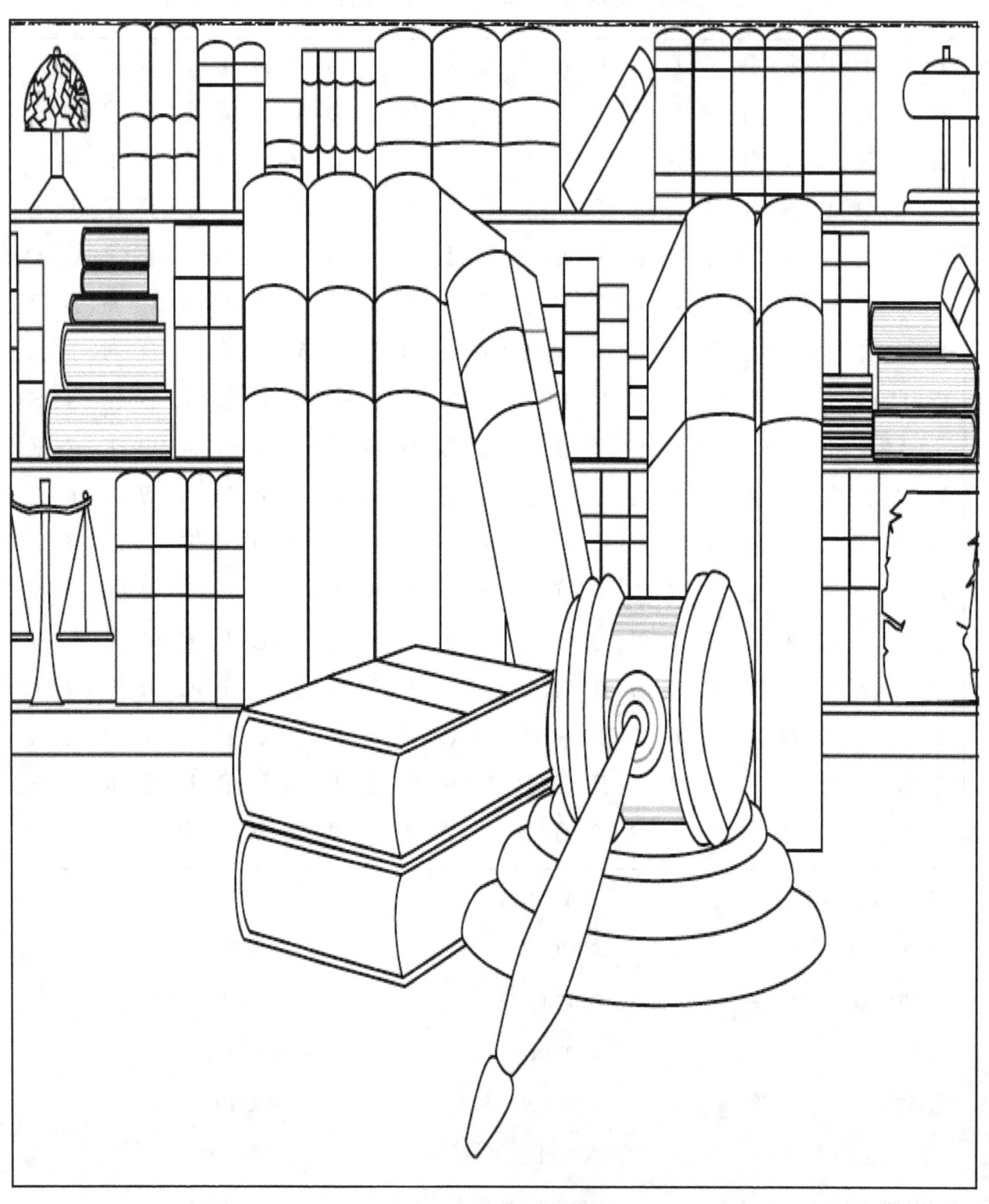

THE JUDGE

FILL IN THE BLANK
COMMIT THESE VERSES OF SCRIPTURE TO MEMORY

_____ TO SHEW THYSELF _____ UNTO GOD, A _____ THAT NEEDETH NOT TO BE _____, RIGHTLY _____ THE WORD OF TRUTH. ~ 2 TIMOTHY 2:15

THUS WILL I CAUSE _____ TO _____ OUT OF THE LAND, THAT ALL _____ MAY BE _____ NOT TO DO AFTER YOUR _____. ~ EZEKIEL 23:48

AND WHEN ABRAM _____ THAT HIS _____ WAS TAKEN _____, HE _____ HIS _____ SERVANTS, _____ IN HIS OWN HOUSE, THREE HUNDRED AND EIGHTEEN, AND _____ THEM UNTO DAN. ~ GENESIS 14:14

NOW WHEN THEY SAW THE _____ OF _____ AND _____, AND PERCEIVED THAT THEY WERE _____ AND _____ MEN, THEY _____; AND THEY TOOK _____ OF THEM, THAT THEY HAD BEEN WITH _____. ~ ACTS 4:13

AND I SAID, HEAR, I _____ YOU, O _____ OF JACOB, AND YE _____ OF THE _____ OF ISRAEL; IS IT NOT FOR YOU TO KNOW _____? ~ MICAH 3:1

_____ NOT _____ ONE OF ANOTHER, BRETHREN. HE THAT _____ _____ OF HIS _____, AND _____ HIS BROTHER, SPEAKETH EVIL OF THE _____, AND _____ THE LAW: BUT IF THOU _____ THE LAW, THOU ART NOT A _____ OF THE LAW, BUT A JUDGE. ~ JAMES 4:11

SECRET MESSAGE 2

A	B	C	D	E	F	G	H	I	J	K	L	M	N	O	P	Q	R	S	T	U	V	W	X	Y	Z
24	8	16	1	15	26	10	3	17	4	13	23	14	7	18	22	6	19	12	25	11	20	2	9	21	5

Use the above keys to decode the message below

23 15 24 19 7   25 18   1 18   2 15 23 23 ,

12 15 15 13   4 11 1 10 14 15 7 25 ,

19 15 23 17 15 20 15   25 3 15

18 22 22 19 15 12 12 15 1 ,   4 11 1 10 15

25 3 15   26 24 25 3 15 19 23 15 12 12 ,

22 23 15 24 1   26 18 19   25 3 15

2 17 1 18 2 .

Where is this text found: _____

Secret Message 2: Answers found on page 37

10

PRINCIPLES IN EDUCATION
CROSSWORD PUZZLE 2

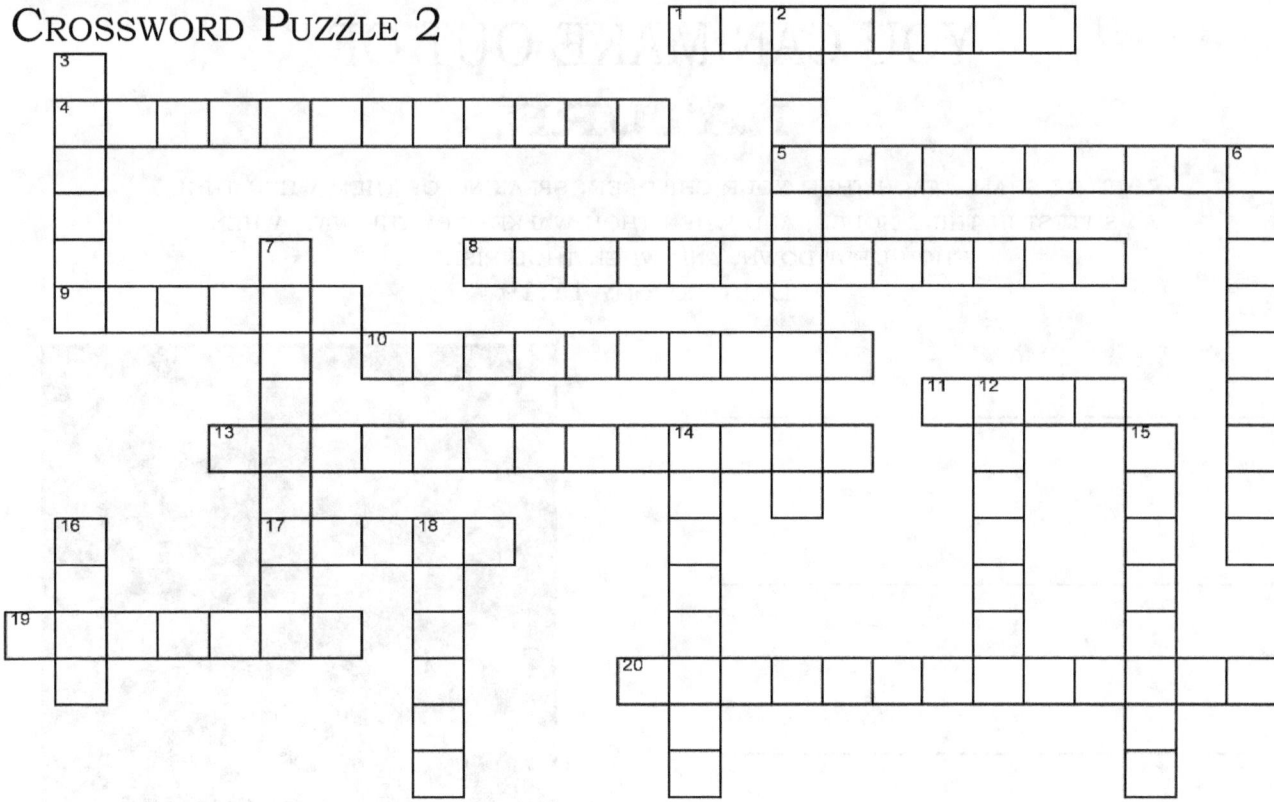

ACROSS

1. TO BE GRANTED AN ACADEMIC DEGREE OR DIPLOMA. ADVANCE TO A NEW LEVEL OF SKILL, ACHIEVEMENT, OR ACTIVITY.

4. LYING OR BEING IN THE MIDDLE PLACE OR DEGREE BETWEEN TWO EXTREMES; INTERVENING; INTERPOSED.

5. THE BODY OF WRITTEN WORKS OF A LANGUAGE, PERIOD, OR CULTURE. IMAGINATIVE OR CREATIVE WRITING.

8. THE STUDENT WITH THE HIGHEST ACADEMIC RANK IN A CLASS WHO DELIVERS THE FAREWELL MESSAGE AT GRADUATION.

9. THE MENTAL FACULTY OF RETAINING AND RECALLING PAST EXPERIENCE. A RETAINING OF PAST IDEAS IN THE MIND.

10. AN INSTITUTION FOR HIGHER LEARNING WITH TEACHING AND RESEARCH FACILITIES THAT AWARD MASTER'S, DOCTORATE'S OR BACHELOR'S DEGREES.

11. A SET OF WRITTEN, PRINTED, OR BLANK PAGES FASTENED ALONG ONE SIDE AND ENCASED BETWEEN PROTECTIVE COVERS.

13. THE ACT OF MAKING OR ARRIVING AT A DECISION. FIRMNESS OF PURPOSE; RESOLVE.

17. CHARACTERIZED BY SHARP QUICK THOUGHT; BRIGHT. ACUTE AND PERTINENT.

19. NARRATION; STORY. AN ACCOUNT OF THE ORIGIN, LIFE AND ACTIONS OF AN INDIVIDUAL PERSON.

20. THE ACT OR FACT OF GRASPING THE MEANING, NATURE, OR IMPORTANCE OF; UNDERSTANDING.

DOWN

2. THE ACT OF PUTTING SOMETHING TO A SPECIAL USE OR PURPOSE. A REQUEST, AS FOR ASSISTANCE, EMPLOYMENT, OR ADMISSION TO A SCHOOL.

3. THE ABILITY TO DISCERN OR JUDGE WHAT IS TRUE, RIGHT, OR LASTING; INSIGHT. COMMON SENSE; GOOD JUDGMENT.

6. PRODUCING A STRONG IMPRESSION OR RESPONSE; STRIKING. HAVING THE POWER OF ACTIVE OPERATION; ABLE.

7. A COLLEGE OR UNIVERSITY TEACHER WHO RANKS ABOVE AN ASSOCIATE PROFESSOR. A TEACHER OR INSTRUCTOR.

12. TO BE OR BECOME AWARE OF, ESPECIALLY THROUGH CAREFUL AND DIRECTED ATTENTION; NOTICE. TO WATCH ATTENTIVELY.

14. THE STUDY OF THE NATURE OF GOD AND RELIGIOUS TRUTH. THE DOCTRINES WE ARE TO BELIEVE, AND THE DUTIES WE ARE TO PRACTICE.

15. THE ACTION FOR WHICH A PERSON OR THING IS PARTICULARLY FITTED OR EMPLOYED. ASSIGNED DUTY OR ACTIVITY.

16. TO TEST THE KNOWLEDGE OF BY POSING QUESTIONS. TO QUESTION CLOSELY OR REPEATEDLY; INTERROGATE.

18. TO BEAR OR BRING BACK AN ANSWER, OR TO RELATE WHAT HAS BEEN DISCOVERED BY A PERSON SENT TO EXAMINE, EXPLORE OR INVESTIGATE.

CROSSWORD PUZZLE 2: ANSWERS FOUND ON PAGE 36

SEE HOW MANY WORDS
YOU CAN MAKE OUT OF
NATURE

"AND YE SHALL TEACH THEM YOUR CHILDREN, SPEAKING OF THEM WHEN THOU
SITTEST IN THINE HOUSE, AND WHEN THOU WALKEST BY THE WAY, WHEN
THOU LIEST DOWN, AND WHEN THOU RISEST UP."
~ DEUTERONOMY 11:19

_____

_____

_____

_____   _____

_____   _____

_____   _____

_____   _____

"FINDING HIS WAY IS KEY IN THE WORD OF GOD"

SEEK AND FIND YOUR WAY THROUGH THE MAZE BELOW

END

START

LINE UPON LINE, PRECEPT UPON PRECEPT, HERE A LITTLE, THERE A LITTLE...

WRITE DOWN YOUR UNDERSTANDING OF EACH WORD FROM THESE BIBLE VERSES

ALTAR – (GENESIS 8:20; GENESIS 22:9; EXODUS 38:1; DEUTERONOMY 27:5; 2 SAMUEL 24:25)

_____

_____

ANOINT – (EXODUS 28:41; EXODUS 30:26; 1 SAMUEL 9:16; 1 SAMUEL 16:12; 1 KINGS 19:16)

_____

_____

BETRAY – (MATTHEW 24:10; MARK 13:12; LUKE 22:4; JOHN 6:64; JOHN 13:11)

_____

_____

BIRTHRIGHT – (GENESIS 25:31-33; GENESIS 27:36; GENESIS 43:33; 1 CHRONICLES 5:1; HEBREWS 12:16)

_____

_____

DESOLATE – (EXODUS 23:29; LEVITICUS 26:22; PSALM 69:25; MATTHEW 23:38; ACTS 1:20)

_____

_____

CHRISTIAN EDUCATION
FIND THESE WORDS IN THE FOREST OF LETTERS

```
A X M J D H J I N T E R M E D I A T E B C P O W U
L K O E H Y G T I X L Y K S E Y R C J X O R G N V
T G L G W G R G M H Y G U X N B J X L N R O O D V
U W O D R O X A P P L I C A T I O N O D Q F K W A
M F F L I N W Y Q J Q G I X D N K I B F X E J Z M
A U U M L M B J X H X R S E V S B S E D S O U B
I N E G B F L K M J O N L I T N C G E A W S Q N W
Z C V R L B Y N E T U M V S E T I V R I C O A I I
W T J P E F F E C T I V E H R N M E V J O R H V N
J I I D E H R I V F E Y E Q M P U H E E L B I E J
J O H T E S D P M T G R J L I T E R A T U R E R U
T N J R F E T O A O P E Y M N S M A R T J N Y S Q
A Q F V L Q D U L M U R P P A B H J B E Y B M I U
R D K A I S D O O D O G V U T E C H X X U X O T I
W V V T I A E C G M Q M N H I S T O R Y X W O Y Z
N X L W R H Y J E Z M T E F O J Z B B O C V K D X
U Y Q G T C A M C T Z E P N N R H R E P O R T Z J
```

APPLICATION	BOOK	COMPREHENSION
DETERMINATION	EFFECTIVE	FUNCTION
GRADUATE	HISTORY	INTERMEDIATE
LITERATURE	MEMORY	OBSERVE
PROFESSOR	QUIZ	REPORT
SMART	THEOLOGY	UNIVERSITY
VALEDICTORIAN	WISDOM	

WORD SEARCH 2: ANSWERS FOUND ON PAGE 35

SECRET MESSAGE 3

A	B	C	D	E	F	G	H	I	J	K	L	M	N	O	P	Q	R	S	T	U	V	W	X	Y	Z
17	6	20	2	21	24	13	4	14	8	22	1	26	7	18	25	9	3	15	23	5	16	10	19	11	12

USE THE ABOVE KEYS TO DECODE THE MESSAGE BELOW

BUT IF ANY WIDOW
6 5 23   14 24   17 7 11   10 14 2 18 10

HAVE CHILDREN OR
4 17 16 21   20 4 14 1 2 3 21 7   18 3

NEPHEWS, LET THEM
7 21 25 4 21 10 15 ,   1 21 23   23 4 21 26

LEARN FIRST TO
1 21 17 3 7   24 14 3 15 23   23 18

SHEW PIETY AT HOME,
15 4 21 10   25 14 21 23 11   17 23   4 18 26 21 ,

AND TO REQUITE THEIR
17 7 2   23 18   3 21 9 5 14 23 21   23 4 21 14 3

PARENTS: FOR THAT IS
25 17 3 21 7 23 15 :   24 18 3   23 4 17 23   14 15

GOOD AND ACCEPTABLE
13 18 18 2   17 7 2   17 20 20 21 25 23 17 6 1 21

BEFORE GOD.
6 21 24 18 3 21   13 18 2 .

WHERE IS THIS TEXT FOUND: _____

MEASURING YOUR EDUCATION
CROSSWORD PUZZLE 3

CROSSWORD PUZZLE 3: ANSWERS FOUND ON PAGE 36

ACROSS

1. THIS WAS THE SMALLEST ROMAN COIN IN USE, EQUAL IN VALUE TO 1/64 OF A DENARIUS. A DENARIUS WAS THE AVERAGE WAGE THAT A WORKER WOULD RECEIVE FOR A DAY'S WORK. (MARK 12:42)

3. IT WAS EQUIVALENT TO 5.1 PINTS. (EXODUS 16:16)

5. THIS WAS LESS THAN ONE HALF OF A PINT. (LEVITICUS 14:10)

7. THIS WAS A DISTANCE OF ABOUT 600 FEET, LESS THAN ONE EIGHTH OF A MILE. (JOHN 6:19)

9. THIS WAS THE NATURAL CAPACITY OF THE HUMAN HAND. (1 KINGS 17:12)

10. THIS WAS THE WIDTH OF THE FOUR FINGERS CLOSELY PRESSED TOGETHER, BETWEEN THREE AND FOUR INCHES. (2CHRONICLES 4:5)

13. THIS WAS THE SMALLEST JEWISH COIN IN USE AND IT WAS ONLY WORTH HALF OF A FARTHING (MARK 12:42)

15. THE WEIGHT FROM ONE THIRD TO ONE HALF OF AN OUNCE. (2 CHRONICLES 1:17)

16. IT WAS 1/6 OF A BATH, APPROXIMATELY A GALLON OR ABOUT FIVE LITERS. (NUMBERS 15:4)

17. EQUIVALENT TO 50 SHEKELS; 20 OZ., OR 571.2 GRAMS. (JOHN 12:3)

DOWN

2. THIS WAS THE LARGEST WEIGHT AMONG THE HEBREWS. ONE OF THESE WAS ABOUT 3000 SHEKELS (ABOUT 90 POUNDS). (2 KINGS 5:23)

4. THIS WAS 1618 YARDS (EIGHT FURLONGS) WHICH IS A LITTLE LESS THAN OUR AMERICAN FURLONGS (1760 YARDS) OR 5,280 FT. (MATTHEW 5:41)

6. THIS WAS THE LENGTH OF THE ARM FROM THE POINT OF THE ELBOW TO THE END OF THE MIDDLE FINGER, WHICH FOR AN ADULT IS ABOUT 17 TO 22 INCHES. (1 SAMUEL 17:4)

7. THIS WAS ABOUT NINE GALLONS (PERHAPS SLIGHTLY LESS). (JOHN 2:6)

8. THIS WAS THE WIDTH FROM THE END OF THE THUMB TO THAT OF THE LITTLE FINGER, WHEN THESE ARE EXTENDED, WHICH FOR AN ADULT IS ABOUT NINE INCHES. (EXODUS 39:9)

11. THIS WAS THE LARGEST LIQUID MEASURE USED BY THE JEWS IN THE OLD TESTAMENT. IT WAS APPROXIMATELY THE AMOUNT OF WATER CARRIED IN A JAR FROM THE WELL BY THE DAUGHTERS IN A HOUSEHOLD ITS CAPACITY WAS ABOUT SIX GALLONS. (EZEKIEL 45:11)

12. ORIGINALLY THIS TERM SIGNIFIED AN JACKASS LOAD (THE AMOUNT A DONKEY COULD CARRY), WHICH WOULD BE LESS THAN EIGHT BUSHELS. (HOSEA 3:2)

14. THIS WAS THE DENARIUS (A ROMAN SILVER COIN), WHICH WAS THE ORDINARY PAY OR WAGES FOR A DAY'S LABOR. (MATTHEW 22:19)

"FINDING HIS WAY IS KEY IN THE WORD OF GOD"
SEEK AND FIND YOUR WAY THROUGH THE MAZE BELOW

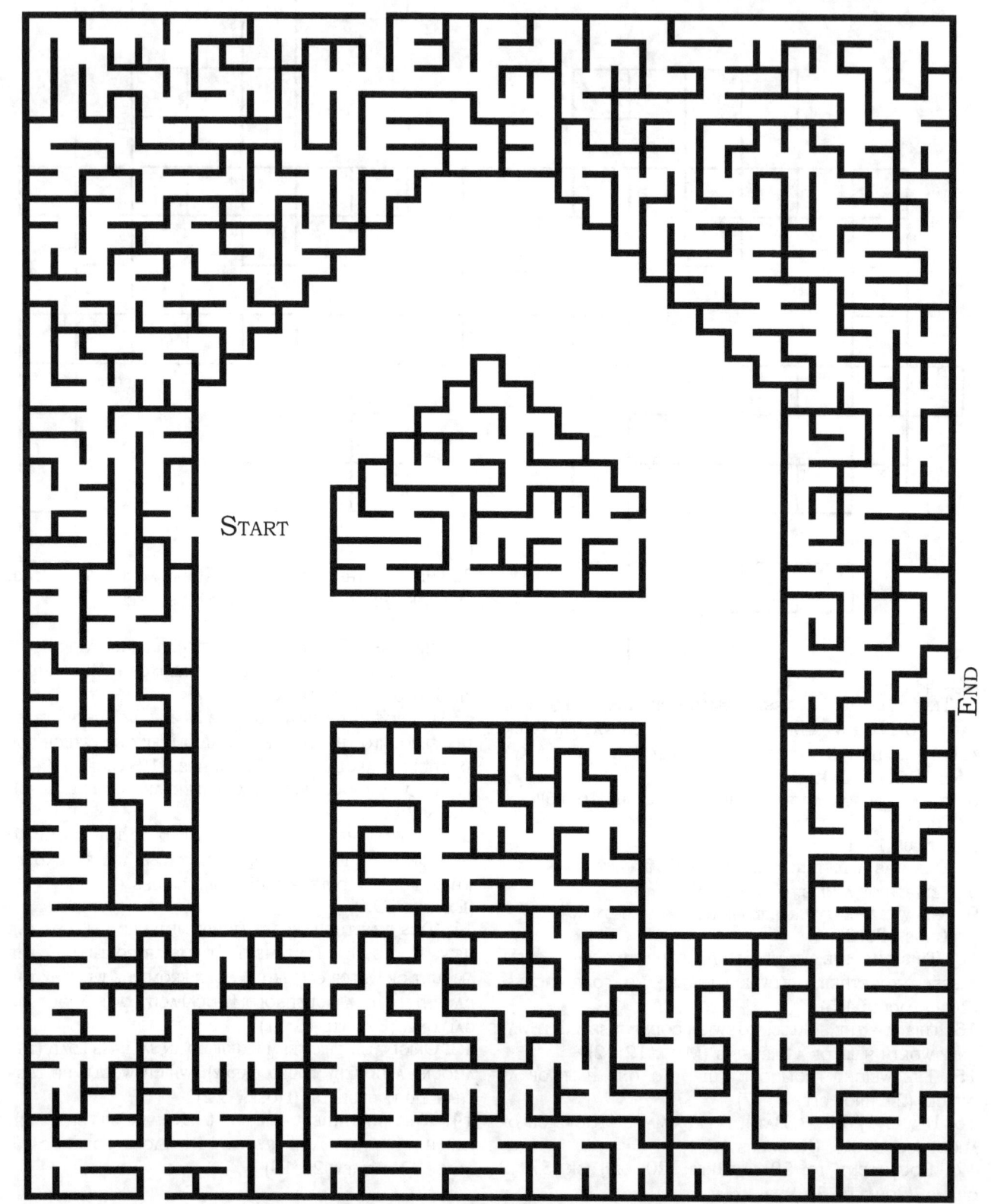

START

END

SEE HOW MANY WORDS
YOU CAN MAKE OUT OF
CLASSROOM

"AND JESUS WENT ABOUT ALL GALILEE, TEACHING IN THEIR SYNAGOGUES, AND PREACHING
THE GOSPEL OF THE KINGDOM, AND HEALING ALL MANNER OF SICKNESS
AND ALL MANNER OF DISEASE AMONG THE PEOPLE."
~ MATTHEW 4:23

_____

_____

_____

_____   _____

_____   _____

_____   _____

_____   _____

BIBLE MEASUREMENTS
FIND THESE WORDS IN THE FOREST OF LETTERS

```
H A N D B R E A D T H V B T H I G D B N C N L B S
Q Q C N M F Z I R R B P O U N D X P J R R F P E J
W D M C E U Z Y L D W S S C A U Y X T Z Q L J O K
J Z I S K R C J Z Z U L P Q L J R K D S A R P E G
P Z L Y C L O D S D S V U A P O B L A C H X E O S
O U E D Y O X V F A R T H I N G G V E Z C S N D B
B G F C Q N G B R Y L S G J S L H H X J B I N G B
M X P E B G H Q B O M O C A S F V A D H L M Y Z S
Q J U B Q S O M Y G J W M O R S G A N J H Z K P H
K J U A Y A M D H R U M K X F J S O T D W F W N E
K K O T C L E O S T A L E N T S S M F W F D N D K
C F E H F I R K I N S M I G J C I E P K F U L M E
X F G E E W A Q J Z E Q X G I A L R I L U C L F L
S S V H W F N B C T U W H B G N A B M L W V C U Q
W Z P I R C P A I N Z I P J L R Q R O C U B I T Q
X V B N I F U M O A T D P V N I E Q D G M O Z J Y
L Z M P B S V R E L B Z P D H J M X Z T G R C U A
```

HANDBREADTH	SPAN	CUBIT	FURLONGS	MILE
HANDFUL	OMER	HOMER	FIRKINS	BATH
HIN	LOG	SHEKEL	TALENT	FARTHING
MITE	PENNY	POUND		

FILL IN THE BLANK
COMMIT THESE BIBLE VERSES TO MEMORY

THY _____ HAVE MADE ME AND _____ ME: GIVE ME UNDERSTANDING, THAT I MAY _____ THY _____. ~ PSALM 119:73

AND THOU SHALT _____ THEM _____ AND _____, AND SHALT _____ THEM THE _____ WHEREIN THEY MUST _____, AND THE _____ THAT THEY MUST DO. ~ EXODUS 18:20

AND HE _____ INTO ONE OF THE _____, WHICH WAS SIMON'S, AND _____ HIM THAT HE WOULD _____ OUT A LITTLE FROM THE LAND. AND HE SAT DOWN, AND _____ THE PEOPLE OUT OF THE SHIP. ~ LUKE 5:3

THE SAME CAME TO _____ BY NIGHT, AND SAID UNTO HIM, _____, WE _____ THAT THOU ART A _____ COME FROM _____: FOR NO MAN CAN DO THESE _____ THAT THOU DOEST, _____ GOD BE WITH HIM. ~ JOHN 3:2

SO THEY _____ IN THE _____ IN THE LAW OF GOD _____, AND GAVE THE _____, AND CAUSED THEM TO _____ THE READING. ~ NEHEMIAH 8:8

SEE HOW MANY WORDS
YOU CAN MAKE OUT OF
STANDARDS

"GO THROUGH, GO THROUGH THE GATES; PREPARE YE THE WAY OF THE PEOPLE; CAST UP, CAST UP THE HIGHWAY; GATHER OUT THE STONES; LIFT UP A STANDARD FOR THE PEOPLE."
~ ISAIAH 62:10

LOVE FAITH

CHRIST

PRAYER

UNSCRAMBLE THE WORDS BELOW
THEN UNSCRAMBLE THE MISSING LETTERS FOR THE WORD BELOW

TUDNIEO _   _____

MERY _ M   _____

SOPREFRO _   _____

CENTE _ ITL   _____

DRAGT _ AE   _____

RE _ VBOS   _____

CR _ SEU   _____

TEDTEAMI   _____

SHRIMPCOENOE _   _____

TREP _ O   _____

__ __ __ __ __ __ __ __ __

"FINDING HIS WAY IS KEY IN THE WORD OF GOD"

SEEK AND FIND YOUR WAY THROUGH THE MAZE BELOW

Start

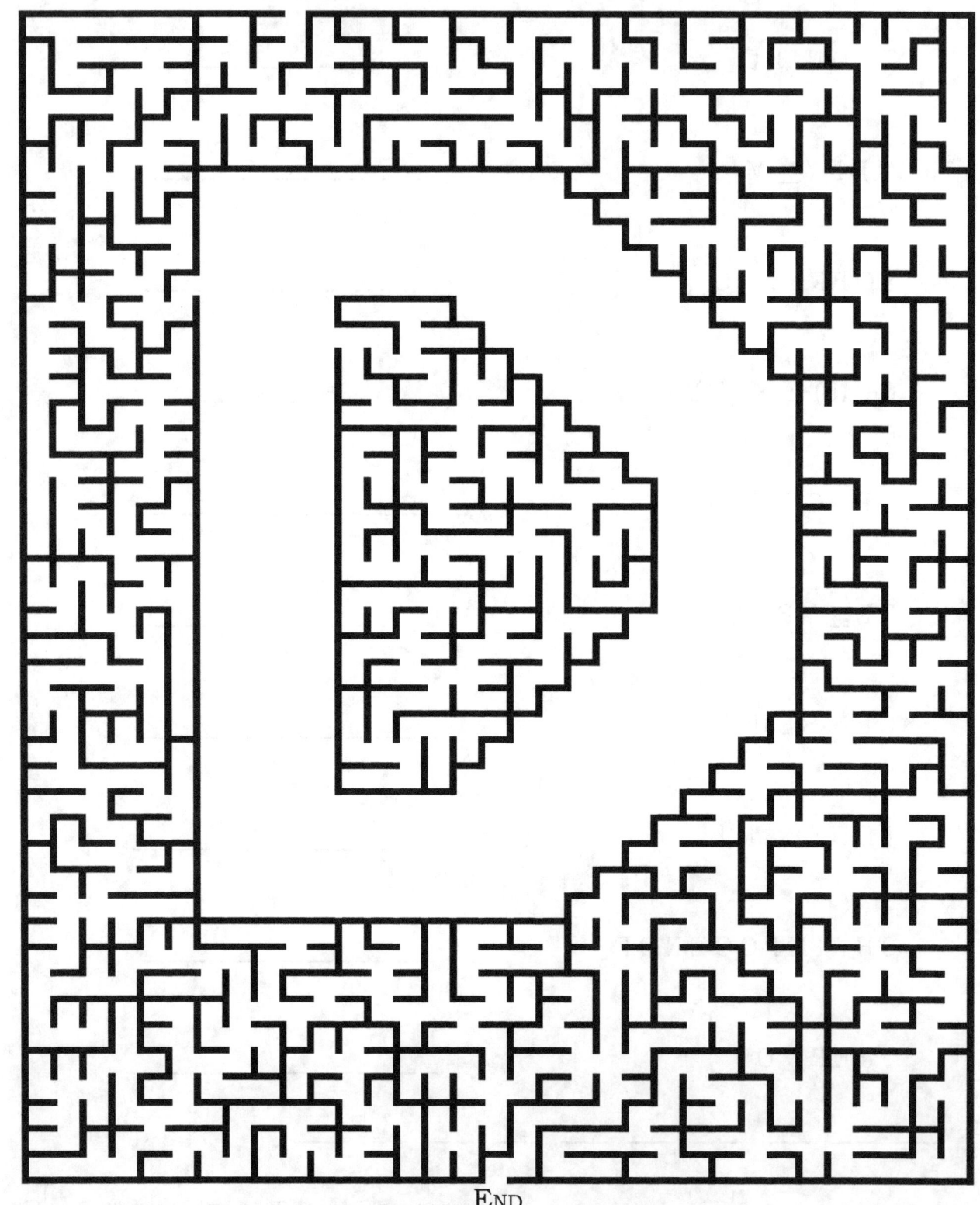

End

EDUCATION IN THE TEMPLE
CROSSWORD PUZZLE 4

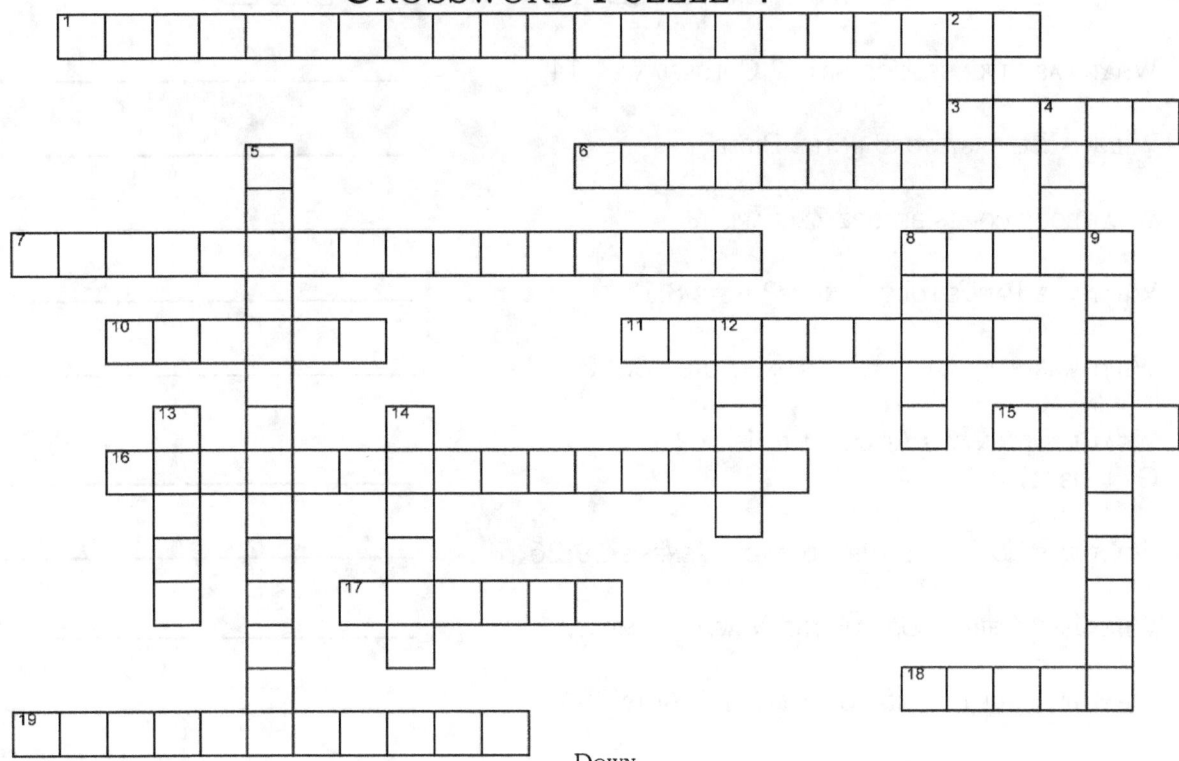

ACROSS

1. A MOUNT; A TABLE OR ELEVATED PLACE, ON WHICH SACRIFICES WHERE ANCIENTLY OFFERED TO SOME DEITY. (EXODUS 30:28)

3. A VESSEL FOR WASHING; A LARGE BASIN. (EXODUS 30:18)

6. LOAVES OF BREAD WHICH THE PRIEST OF THE WEEK PLACED BEFORE THE LORD, ON THE GOLDEN TABLE IN THE SANCTUARY. (EXODUS 25:30)

7. A SMALL CLOSED VESSEL, CHEST OR COFFER, SUCH AS THAT WHICH WAS THE REPOSITORY OF THE TABLES OF THE COVENANT AMONG THE JEWS. (NUMBERS 10:33)

8. A CONCAVE VESSEL TO HOLD LIQUORS, MORE WIDE THAN DEEP; A BASIN. (EXODUS 25:29)

10. A FIGURE COMPOSED OF VARIOUS CREATURES, AS A MAN, AN OX, AN EAGLE OR LION. THEY HAD THE LIKENESS OF A MAN. (EXODUS 25:19)

11. THE FIRST COMPARTMENT OF THE TABERNACLE, WHERE THE PRIEST MINISTER. (EXODUS 28:43)

15. A LARGE DOOR WHICH GIVES ENTRANCE INTO A WALLED CITY, A CASTLE, A TEMPLE, PALACE OR OTHER LARGE EDIFICE. (EXODUS 27:16)

16. THE SECOND COMPARTMENT OF THE TABERNACLE WHERE THE SHEKINAH GLORY APPEARS. (HEBREWS 9:3)

17. A VASE OR PAN IN WHICH INCENSE IS BURNED. A KIND OF CHAFING-DISH, USED TO OFFER PERFUMES IN SACRIFICES. (LEVITICUS 16:12)

18. A PIECE OF TIMBER SAWED THIN AND OF CONSIDERABLE LENGTH AND BREADTH, COMPARED WITH THE THICKNESS, USED FOR BUILDING AND OTHER PURPOSES. (EXODUS 26:17)

19. AN INSTRUMENT OR UTENSIL TO HOLD A CANDLE, MADE IN DIFFERENT FORMS AND OF DIFFERENT MATERIALS. (EXODUS 25:31)

DOWN

2. A PRECIOUS METAL OF A BRIGHT YELLOW COLOR, AND THE MOST EASILY MOLDED OR SHAPED OF ALL THE METALS. (EXODUS 25:11)

4. A COVER; A CURTAIN; SOMETHING TO INTERCEPT THE VIEW AND HIDE AN OBJECT. (EXODUS 30:6)

5. A RAISED PLACE OR STRUCTURE WHERE ODORS OF SPICES ARE BURNT AS AN OFFERING IN A RELIGIOUS RITE. (1 CHRONICLES 28:18)

8. A YELLOWISH ALLOY OF COPPER AND ZINC, SOMETIMES INCLUDING SMALL AMOUNTS OF OTHER METALS, BUT USUALLY 67 PERCENT COPPER AND 33 PERCENT ZINC. (EXODUS 26:11)

9. BOARDS OF THE TABERNACLE WERE MADE AMONG THE JEWS. THIS WOOD IS SAID TO BE HARD, TOUGH AND SMOOTH, AND VERY BEAUTIFUL. (EXODUS 25:10)

12. CLOTH MADE OF FLAX OR HEMP. (EXODUS 26:1)

13. IN SCRIPTURE, IT IS A SYMBOL OF STRENGTH OR POWER. (EXODUS 27:2)

14. A THIN NARROW PIECE OF TIMBER, OF WHICH CASKS ARE MADE. A STAFF; A METRICAL PORTION. (EXODUS 25:13)

CROSSWORD PUZZLE 4: ANSWERS FOUND ON PAGE 36

BIBLE TRIVIA
Use capital letters when needed

WHAT WAS LUKE BY PROFESSION? COLOSSIANS 4:14

_____

WHAT IS THE LAST WORD IN THE BIBLE?

_____

WHAT BOOK COMES BEFORE ZECHARIAH?

_____

WHAT WAS PAUL'S FORMER NAME? ACTS 8:1

_____

WHAT WAS AQUILA BY PROFESSION? ACTS 18:2,3

_____

WHAT RELATION WAS ABRAHAM TO ISAAC?
GENESIS 21:3

_____

WHAT WAS LOT'S WIFE TURNED INTO? GENESIS 19:26

_____

WHAT IS THE FIRST BOOK OF THE NEW TESTAMENT?

_____

WHAT BIT PAUL BUT DID NOT HARM HIM? ACTS 28:3

_____

WHAT DOES THE ABBREVIATION O.T. STAND FOR?

_____

WHAT ARE THE STREETS OF HEAVEN PAVED WITH?
REVELATION 21:21

_____

WHAT DID NOAH BUILD? GENESIS 6:14

_____

WHAT BOOK IN THE O.T. STARTS WITH A?

_____

WHAT WERE JESUS' LAST WORDS AT HIS DEATH? JOHN 19:30

_____

WHAT TREE DID JESUS CURSE? MATTHEW 21:19

_____

WHAT WAS JESUS' FIRST BED? LUKE 2:7

_____

WHAT STOOD STILL FOR JOSHUA? JOSHUA 10:13

_____

WHAT BOOKS IN THE BIBLE BEGINS WITH Z?

_____

WHAT TYPE OF BIRD WAS EATEN IN THE WILDERNESS?
EXODUS 16:13

_____

WHAT IS THE LAST WORD IN THE O.T.?

_____

BIBLE TRIVIA: ANSWERS FOUND ON PAGE 34

EDUCATION IN THE SANCTUARY
FIND THESE WORDS IN THE FOREST OF LETTERS

```
W L M I H V H D J O T D H X W M U B G O L D A W R
O A U D U X T O M L D U U C D W F B R A S S A B Y
O L U O C A N D L E S T I C K I S A F J L V M O V
F T P R T N D M J Z C B O B S H E W B R E A D A T
P A H O L I E S T O F H O L I E S A F B S Y E R G
X R C H U D T L Z M H U R S F Q I K R K I Z R D Y
X O T C W F H X P B C S C W V N A U E T P G M C D
C F P C H O R N S J L I S F P R U T V R T A L I K
Z I Z P E V L S Y Z A M U Z M Q A G Y Q B N I V Z
A N B J S N E B D J V X E C R G C K A B B V N X X
A C C G X V S U S N E S H I T T I M W O O D E J G
R E G D A E T E C H R S O L U X Y K G X I Z N J I
W N Y T W F D O R X L T W H O L Y P L A C E R D R
A S S I M L N I G W V E T P O Y F P Q W E X D L F
Y E X P I F B F O Z R V L Z B R A S E N A L T A R
A Q Z A O V D B C H E R U B P Z M W L Y L M P Z U
O W V F C A R K O F T H E C O V E N A N T E X D N
```

LAVER	GOLD	BRASEN ALTAR
ALTAR OF INCENSE	BRASS	ARK OF THE COVENANT
VAIL	HOLY PLACE	SHEWBREAD
CANDLESTICK	SHITTIM WOOD	GATE
CHERUB	LINEN	STAVES
BOWLS	HOLIEST OF HOLIES	HORNS
CENSER	BOARD	

SEE HOW MANY WORDS
YOU CAN MAKE OUT OF
TEACHER

"THE SAME CAME TO JESUS BY NIGHT, AND SAID UNTO HIM, RABBI, WE KNOW THAT THOU
ART A TEACHER COME FROM GOD: FOR NO MAN CAN DO THESE MIRACLES
THAT THOU DOEST, EXCEPT GOD BE WITH HIM."
~ JOHN 3:2

_____

_____

_____

_____   _____

_____   _____

_____   _____

_____   _____

SECRET MESSAGE 3

A	B	C	D	E	F	G	H	I	J	K	L	M	N	O	P	Q	R	S	T	U	V	W	X	Y	Z
12	22	4	17	3	14	24	16	5	18	1	11	2	21	6	10	20	7	26	13	25	8	15	23	9	19

USE THE ABOVE KEYS TO DECODE THE MESSAGE BELOW

```
___  ___  ___  ___      ___  ___  ___  ___  ___      ___  ___  ___      ___  ___  ___  ___ ,
13   16   25   26       26   12   5    13   16       13   16   3        11   6    7    17
```

```
___  ___  ___  ___  ___      ___  ___  ___      ___  ___  ___      ___  ___  ___
11   3    12   7    21       21   6    13       13   16   3        15   12   9
```

```
___  ___      ___  ___  ___      ___  ___  ___  ___  ___  ___  ___ ,     ___  ___  ___
6    16       13   16   3        16   3    12   13   16   3    21        12   21   17
```

```
___  ___      ___  ___  ___      ___  ___  ___  ___  ___  ___  ___  ___      ___  ___
22   3        21   6    13       17   5    26   2    12   9    3    17       12   13
```

```
___  ___  ___      ___  ___  ___  ___  ___      ___  ___      ___  ___  ___  ___  ___  ___ ;
13   16   3        26   5    24   21   26       6    14       16   3    12   8    3    21
```

```
___  ___  ___      ___  ___  ___      ___  ___  ___  ___  ___  ___  ___      ___  ___  ___
14   6    7        13   16   3        16   3    12   13   16   3    21       12   7    3
```

```
___  ___  ___  ___  ___  ___  ___  ___      ___  ___      ___  ___  ___  ___ .
17   5    26   2    12   9    3    17       12   13       13   16   3    2
```

WHERE IS THIS TEXT FOUND: _____

SECRET MESSAGE 4: ANSWERS FOUND ON PAGE 37

LINE UPON LINE, PRECEPT UPON PRECEPT, HERE A LITTLE, THERE A LITTLE...

WRITE DOWN YOUR UNDERSTANDING OF THESE VERSES

2 TIMOTHY 3:14-17

_____

_____

2 TIMOTHY 2:15

_____

_____

MATTHEW 13:47-52

_____

_____

DEUTERONOMY 4:9-10

_____

_____

MATTHEW 24:36

_____

_____

2 TIMOTHY 3:14-17

_____

_____

COLORING ACTIVITY

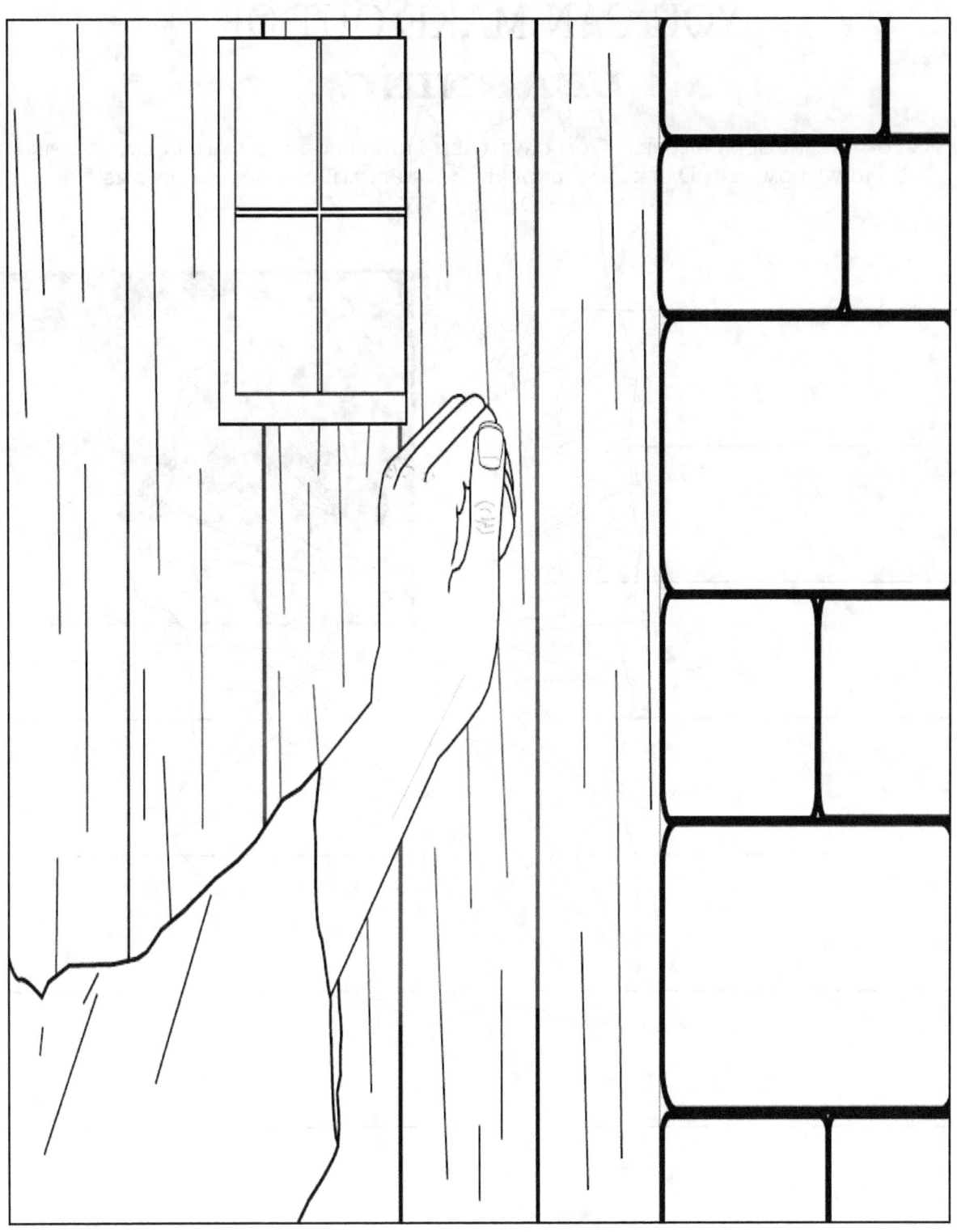

THE KNOCK

SEE HOW MANY WORDS
YOU CAN MAKE OUT OF
LEARNING

"As for these four children, God gave them knowledge and skill in all learning and wisdom: and Daniel had understanding in all visions and dreams."
~ Daniel 1:17

_____

_____

_____

_____   _____

_____   _____

_____   _____

_____   _____

LINE UPON LINE, PRECEPT UPON PRECEPT, HERE A LITTLE, THERE A LITTLE...

WRITE DOWN YOUR UNDERSTANDING OF EACH WORD FROM THESE BIBLE VERSES

Guile – (John 1:47; 2 Corinthians 12:16; 1 Thessalonians 2:3; 1 Peter 2:22; Revelations 14:5)

_____

_____

Magnify – (Joshua 3:7; Psalm 34:3; Psalm 69:30; Isaiah 42:21; Luke 1:46)

_____

_____

Nature – (Romans 2:14; Romans 11:24; Galatians 2:15; Ephesians 2:3; 2 Peter 1:4)

_____

_____

Repentance – (Luke 15:7; Acts 19:4; Romans 2:4; 2 Corinthians 7:9,10; Hebrews 6:1,6)

_____

_____

Reprove – (Job 6:25; Psalm 50:8; Proverbs 9:8; Proverbs 19:25; Isaiah 11:3,4)

_____

_____

ANSWER PAGES

Bible Trivia

What was Luke by profession?	PHYSICIAN/DOCTOR
What is the last word in the Bible?	AMEN
What book comes before Zechariah?	HAGGAI
What was Paul's former name?	SAUL
What was Aquila by profession?	TENTMAKER
What relation was Abraham to Isaac?	FATHER
What was Lot's wife turned into?	PILLAR OF SALT
What is the first book of the New Testament?	MATTHEW
What bit Paul but did not harm him?	VIPER/SNAKE
What does the abbreviation O.T. stand for?	OLD TESTAMENT
What are the streets of heaven paved with?	PURE GOLD
What did Noah build? Genesis 6:14	AN ARK
What book in the O.T. starts with A?	AMOS
What were Jesus' last words at his death?	IT IS FINISHED
What tree did Jesus curse?	FIG TREE
What was Jesus' first bed?	A MANGER
What stood still for Joshua?	THE SUN
What books in the Bible begins with Z?	ZEPHANIAH & ZECHARIAH
What type of bird was eaten in the wilderness?	QUAIL
What is the last word in the O.T.?	CURSE

WORD SEARCH 1

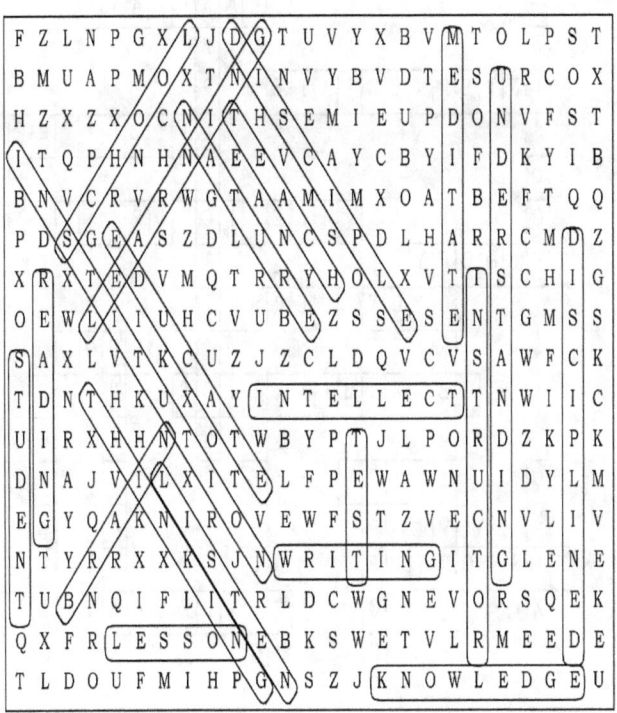

```
F Z L N P G X L J D G T U V Y X B V M T O L P S T
B M U A P M O X T N I N V Y B V D T E S U R C O X
H Z X Z X O C N I T H S E M I E U P D O N V F S T
I T Q P H N H A E E V C A Y C B Y I F D K Y I B
B N V C R V R W G T A A M I M X O A T B E F T Q Q
P D S G E A S Z D L U N C S P D L H A R R C M D Z
X R X T E D V M Q T R R Y H O L X V T S C H I G
O E W L I I U H C V U B E Z S S E S E N T G M S S
S A X L V T K C U Z J Z C L D Q V C S A W F C K
T D N T H K U X A Y I N T E L L E C T T N W I I C
U I R X H H N T O T W B Y P T J L P O R D Z K P K
D N A J V I L X I T E L F P E W A W N U I D Y L M
E G Y Q A K N I R O V E W F S T Z V E C N V L I V
N T Y R R X X S J N W R I T I N G I T G L E N E
T U B N Q I F L I T R L D C W G N E V O R S Q E K
Q X F R L E S S O N E B K S W E T V L R M E E D E
T L D O U F M I H P G N S Z J K N O W L E D G E U
```

WORD SEARCH 2

```
A X M J D H J I N T E R M E D I A T E B C P O W U
L K O E H Y G T I X L Y K S E Y R C J X O R G N V
T G L G W G R G M H Y G U X N B J X L N O O D V
U W O D R O X A P P L I C A T I O N O D Q F K W A
M F F L I N W Y Q J Q G I X D N K I B F X E J Z M
A U U M L M B J X H X R J S E V S B S E D S O U B
I N E G B F L K M J O N L I T N C G E A W S Q N W
Z C V R L B Y N E T U M V S E T I V R I C O A I I
W T J P E F F E C T I V E H R N M E V J O R H V N
J I I D E H R I V F E Y E Q M P U H E E L B I E J
J O H T E S D P M T G R J L I T E R A T U R E R U
T N J R F E T O A O P E Y M N S M A R T J N Y S Q
A Q F V L Q D U L M U R P P A B H J B E Y B M I U
R D K A I S D O O D O G V U T E C H X X U X O T I
W V V T I A E C G M Q M N H I S T O R Y X W O Y Z
N X L W R H Y J E Z M T E F O J Z B B O C V K D X
U Y Q G T C A M C T Z E P N N R H R E P O R T Z J
```

WORD SEARCH 3

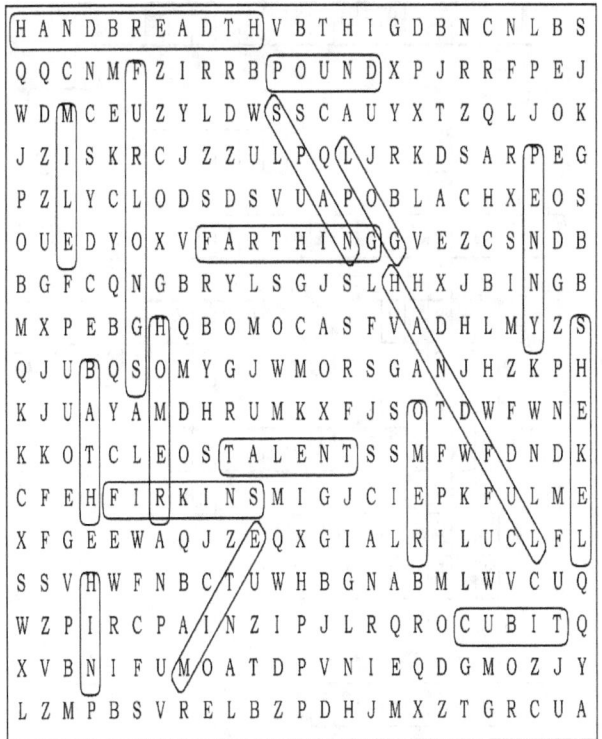

```
H A N D B R E A D T H V B T H I G D B N C N L B S
Q Q C N M F Z I R R B P O U N D X P J R R F P E J
W D M C E U Z Y L D W S S C A U Y X T Z Q L J O K
J Z I S K R C J Z Z U L P Q L J R K D S A R P E G
P Z L Y C L O D S D S V U A P O B L A C H X E O S
O U E D Y O X V F A R T H I N G G V E Z C S N D B
B G F C Q N G B R Y L S G J S L H H X J B I N G B
M X P E B G H Q B O M O C A S F V A D H L M Y Z S
Q J U B Q S O M Y G J W M O R S G A N J H Z K P H
K J U A Y A M D H R U M K X F J S O T D W F W N E
K K O T C L E O S T A L E N T S S M F W F D N D K
C F E H F I R K I N S M I G J C I E P K F U L M E
X F G E E W A Q J Z E Q X G I A L R I L U C L F L
S S V H W F N B C T U W H B G N A B M L W V C U Q
W Z P I R C P A I N Z I P J L R Q R O C U B I T Q
X V B N I F U M O A T D P V N I E Q D G M O Z J Y
L Z M P B S V R E L B Z P D H J M X Z T G R C U A
```

WORD SEARCH 4

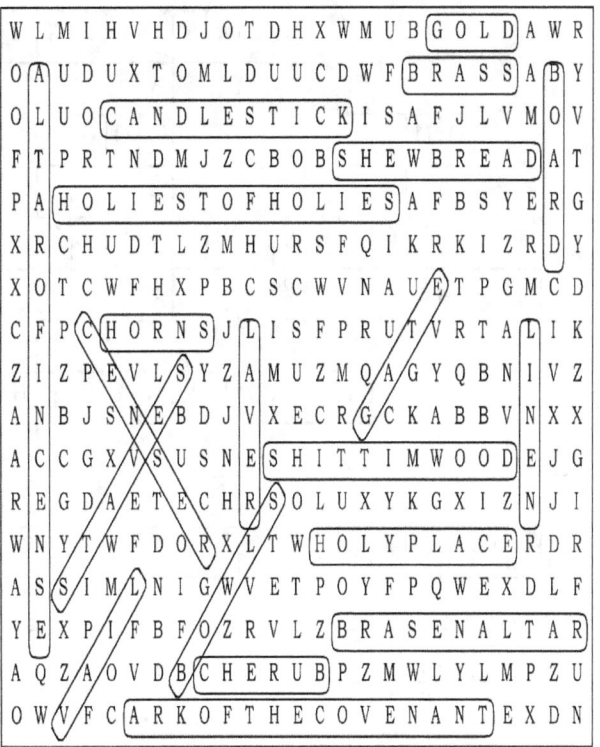

```
W L M I H V H D J O T D H X W M U B G O L D A W R
O A U D U X T O M L D U U C D W F B R A S S A B Y
O L U O C A N D L E S T I C K I S A F J L V M O V
F T P R T N D M J Z C B O B S H E W B R E A D A T
P A H O L I E S T O F H O L I E S A F B S Y E R G
X R C H U D T L Z M H U R S F Q I K R K I Z R D Y
X O T C W F H X P B C S C W V N A U E T P G M C D
C F P C H O R N S J L I S F P R U T V R T A L I K
Z I Z P E V L S Y Z A M U Z M Q A G Y Q B N I V Z
A N B J S N E B D J V X E C R G C K A B B V N X X
A C C G X V S U S N E S H I T T I M W O O D E J G
R E G D A E T E C H R S O L U X Y K G X I Z N J I
W N Y T W F D O R X L T W H O L Y P L A C E R D R
A S S I M L N I G W V E T P O Y F P Q W E X D L F
Y E X P I F B F O Z R V L Z B R A S E N A L T A R
A Q Z A O V D B C H E R U B P Z M W L Y L M P Z U
O W V F C A R K O F T H E C O V E N A N T E X D N
```

CROSSWORD 1

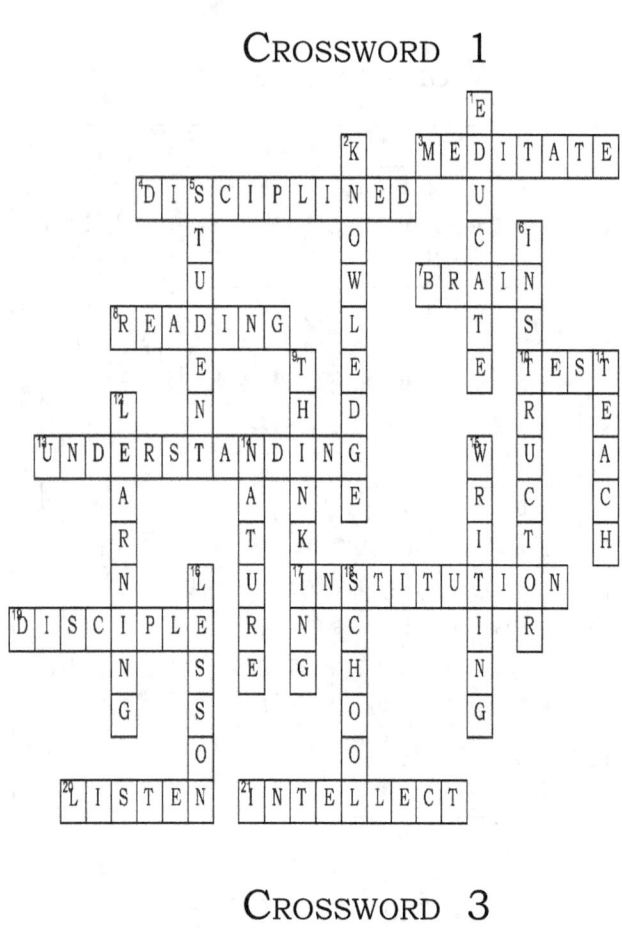

CROSSWORD 2

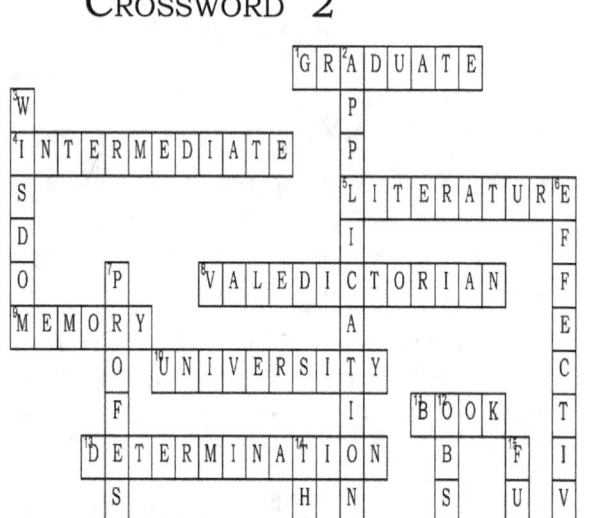

CROSSWORD 3

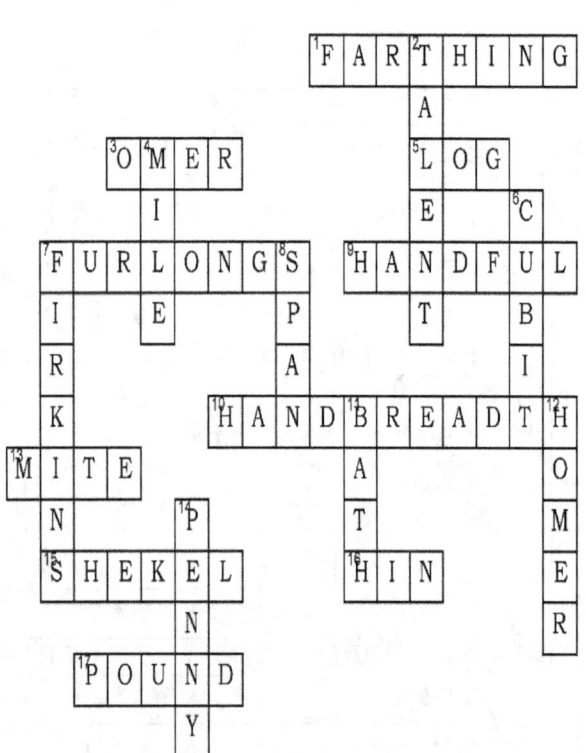

CROSSWORD 4

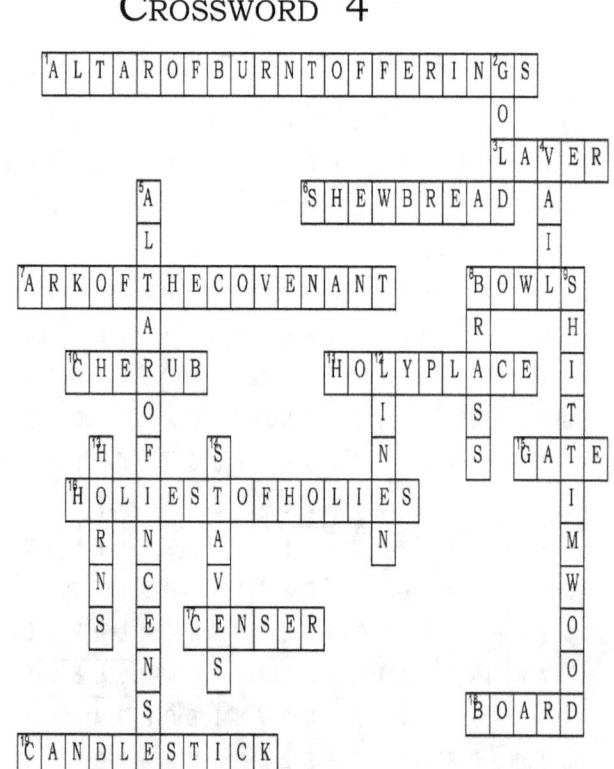

Secret Message 1

Take my yoke upon you, and learn of me; for I am meek and lowly in heart: and ye shall find rest unto your souls.

Matthew 11:29

Secret Message 2

Learn to do well; seek judgment, relieve the oppressed, judge the fatherless, plead for the widow.

Isaiah 1:17

Secret Message 3

But if any widow have children or nephews, let them learn first to shew piety at home, and to requite their parents: for that is good and acceptable before God.

1 Timothy 5:4

Secret Message 4

Thus saith the Lord, Learn not the way of the heathen, and be not dismayed at the signs of heaven; for the heathen are dismayed at them.

Jeremiah 10:2

Unscramble Exercise 1

LOWGEENDK	KNOWLEDGE
DISRUNATEGNDN	UNDERSTANDING
REALN	LEARN
HATCERE	TEACHER
OSMIDW	WISDOM
UTTONSINTII	INSTITUTION
GRITWIN	WRITING
SHIRTOY	HISTORY
NUTDSET	STUDENT
TRUENA	NATURE

E D U C A T I O N

Unscramble Exercise 2

TUDNIEOC	EDUCATION
MERYOM	MEMORY
SOPREFROS	PROFESSOR
CENTELITL	INTELLECT
DRAGTUAE	GRADUATE
REEVBOS	OBSERVE
CROSEU	COURSE
TEDTEAMI	MEDITATE
SHRIMPCOENOEN	COMPREHENSION
TREPRO	REPORT

C O U N S E L L O R

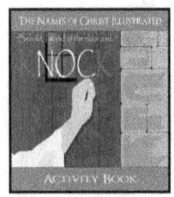

THE NOC ILLUSTRATED
ACTIVITY BOOK

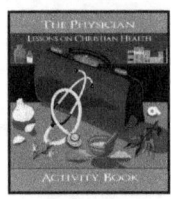

THE PHYSICIAN:
CHRISTIAN HEALTH

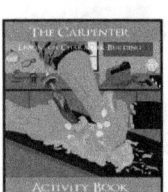

THE CARPENTER:
CHARACTER BUILDING

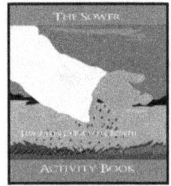

THE SOWER:
CHRISTIAN GROWTH

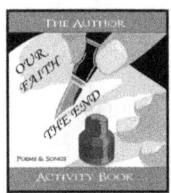

THE AUTHOR:
POEMS & SONGS

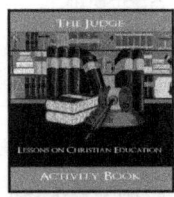

THE JUDGE:
CHRISTIAN EDUCATION

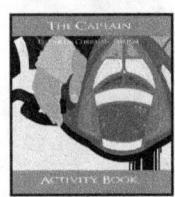

THE CAPTAIN:
CHRISTIAN PURPOSE

"PORTRAITS OF THE SAVIOUR'S
DESIRE TO ENTER HEARTS."

THIS BOOK:

THE JUDGE

LESSONS ON CHRISTIAN EDUCATION

THE NAMES OF CHRIST ILLUSTRATED

PLEASE VISIT US ONLINE TO VIEW
MORE GREAT TITLES AT:

WWW.THENOCILLUSTRATED.COM

www.ingramcontent.com/pod-product-compliance
Lightning Source LLC
Chambersburg PA
CBHW081239170526
45165CB00009B/3115